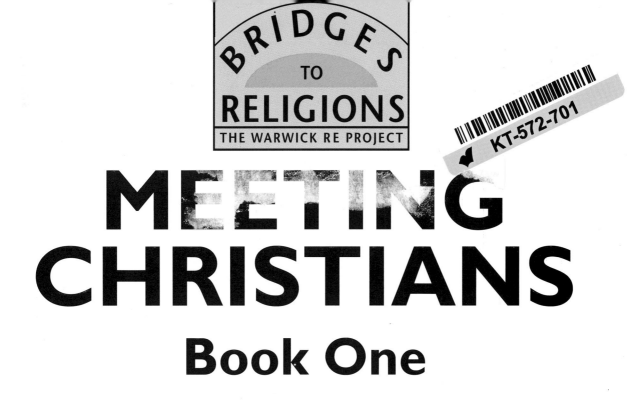

BRIDGES TO RELIGIONS
THE WARWICK RE PROJECT

MEETING CHRISTIANS
Book One

Written by Margaret Barratt and Jo Price
Series editors Judith Everington and Robert Jackson

The authors and publishers would like to thank the members, friends and children of the Rugby United Reformed Church who made the book possible and especially the Hatcher and Burns families, the Rev Derek Hopkins, Mrs Lorna Maloney, Mrs Myra Skinner and the Rev Graham Long; the members of the Salvation Army at the Coventry corps who have been so helpful and welcoming: Dean Heeley, Major and Mrs Heeley, Glenys Marklew, Beverley Parkinson, Claire Whitmore, Alison Potter, and Ian and Maureen Potter.

Heinemann Educational Publishers
Halley Court, Jordan Hill, Oxford OX2 8EJ
a division of Reed Educational & Professional Publishing Ltd.

MADRID ATHENS FLORENCE PRAGUE
PORTSMOUTH NH CHICAGO SAO PAULO MEXICO
SINGAPORE TOKYO MELBOURNE AUCKLAND
IBADAN GABORONE JOHANNESBURG

First published 1996

00 99 98 97 96

10 9 8 7 6 5 4 3 2 1

British Library Cataloguing in Publication Data
A catalogue record for this book is available from the British Library

1 title x 6 copies: ISBN 0 435 30421 6

Key Stage Two Starter Pack: ISBN 0 435 30416 X

Designed and typeset by Tim Peagram Design
Illustrated by Andrew Greenwood, Barrie Richard and Lynne Willey
Cover photographs by Margaret and Noel Barratt
Printed and bound by Mateu Cromo, Spain

Acknowledgements

The authors and publishers would like to thank the following for permission to use photographs/copyright material: V T Forster, p6 (drawing of church); Circa Photo Library, p9 (all); The Guide Association, p11 (top), p16 (Brownie prayer), p20 (reference for badges); National Christian Education Centre, p13 (top); The World Association of Girl Guides and Girl Scouts, p23 (reference for badge); Scripture Union, p28 (worksheet); The Salvation Army, pp29 (both), 31.

Photograph on p20 reproduced by permission of The Bible Societies/HarperCollins Publishers Ltd.

All other photographs by Margaret and Noel Barratt, and courtesy of the young people and their families.

The publishers have made every effort to trace the copyright holders, but if they have inadvertently overlooked any, they will be pleased to make the necessary arrangements at the first opportunity.

Contents

Christians

Have you ever met a **Christian**? The chances are you wouldn't know unless they told you. Christians come in all shapes and sizes, colours and ages.

Sometimes they wear a sign to show they are Christian. It might be a cross or a fish.

Some Christians wear special clothing, but most of the time there is no special way to recognize a Christian.

Christians are people who follow the teachings of **Jesus** of Nazareth. They would say that if you look at Jesus and the way he lived you can see what God is like. They try to live like Jesus. Their special book, the **Bible**, helps them to do this.

There are Christians all over the world. The first ones lived in Israel 2,000 years ago. From there they spread to every country.

They are like one huge family, called the **Church**. Like most families not all Christians do things in the same way.

No one knows exactly what Jesus looked like so they make their own pictures.

In the Christian family there are lots of branches with different names. If you look at churches in your area you may find Orthodox, Roman Catholic, Church of England or Pentecostal, and these are only a few.

Different kinds of Christians

The United Reformed Church

One branch is the United Reformed Church. A United Reformed Church usually has a **minister** who leads and teaches the people, a church secretary who is the main organiser and **elders** who are chosen to help all of the people. Other adults and children have an important part to play in the church too.

Ellie belongs to the United Reformed Church.

The United Reformed Church

The Salvation Army

Another branch is the Salvation Army. It was founded by William Booth over a hundred years ago. He introduced a uniform for members to wear.

Members of the Salvation Army can still choose to wear a uniform if they wish. The ministers in charge are called **officers** and the members are called **soldiers**.

A Salvation Army band often marches to open-air meetings where anyone can join in the singing. The Salvation Army helps many people who are hungry or homeless.

The Salvation Army

Dean belongs to the Salvation Army.

5

Ellie

My name is Eleanor but nearly everyone calls me Ellie. I live with my mum and dad and two sisters. We're a Christian family.

On Sundays we go to the United Reformed Church. I enjoy going there. The minister is interesting but he makes us laugh too. I meet my friend, Nancy, and a crowd of others. The church is a kind of big family that all of us, children and adults, belong to.

My friends and I are old enough to belong to groups at church without our parents.

During part of the Sunday **service**, the church family splits into different groups. We children go to our own groups in the Junior Church then. Nancy and I go to **Brownies** on Tuesdays. I belong to the Youth Club too.

My mum says:

'I want Ellie to feel she belongs to a wider family than just us, to have a feeling of warmth and love from others.'

Jesus said, 'Let the children come to me,' so our church wants us to be partners with the grown-ups in everything that goes on.

Dean

My name is Dean and I am a Christian. I live with my mum, dad, brother and sister. My brother and sister are both older than me. I like football and playing on my computer.

We all belong to a Christian group called the Salvation Army. It's not an army with soldiers who fight with guns, but people and groups have army names. Many of them wear a uniform.

I belong to Junior Soldiers

Mum and Dad at Sunday meeting

My mum and dad are called **Major** and Mrs Heeley. They are in charge of a big Salvation Army group called a **corps**.

I am a Junior Soldier in the Salvation Army and I belong to some church groups. I belong to Sunday School, the Young People's Singing Company and the Youth Club.

I go to church every Sunday.

Our church building is called a **citadel**. I really enjoy taking part in all the activities. It's just like being part of a big, happy family.

The Young People's Singing Company

7

Ellie's Groups

Ellie's church is a bright modern building. On Sunday morning people arrive on foot, in cars or even on bikes, but it isn't only on Sunday that Christians are Christians. It's every day. The church has activities almost every day – some for adults and some for children.

These are the groups Ellie belongs to at church.

The Junior Church

Lorna is the leader of the whole Junior Church. There are several groups. Ellie's is called the Adventurers. The children have their own special room with things they need.

Lorna believes:

'The children should have a say in planning what they do in Junior Church.'

They talk or paint or make things as they learn. Sometimes they put on an exhibition for the adults, to show what they have done.

The adults think it's important for children to be part of the church. The children need to know that they are part of the church – not the only part or the most important part, but an equal part with everyone else.

TEACHER'S RESOURCE BOOK Photocopy sheets 5, 9, 10, 15, 25, 26 accompany this section

The Youth Club

The Youth Club is for junior aged children.

'It's brilliant at club. You can wear what you want. You don't have to be posh! You pay some money to help buy equipment. There are drinks and snacks to buy and loads of things to do.'

The minister says:

'The church wants to help children to enjoy themselves.'

The Brownie Guider says:

'Although we do Brownies at church, you don't have to be a Christian to be a Brownie. Preena is a Hindu. She's a Sprite, like Nancy. Everyone is welcome.'

Brownies

Brownie meetings are fun too, but different.
Brownies wear uniform but they can choose which uniform clothing to wear. The Brownie pack is split into Sixes. They are like teams. Ellie is a Gnome, Nancy is a Sprite.

Ellie says:

'We all get together and do badges together. People come to help us.'

What groups do you belong to without your family?

What do you like about your group?

How is it like the groups here and how is it different?

Gnome

Sprite

9

Joining

There are some groups that Ellie has always belonged to and others which she has chosen to belong to.

Junior Church

Ellie didn't have to join the Junior Church. She had been part of the church since she was **baptized** as a baby. In the Junior Church you change groups as you get older.

Now Ellie's an Adventurer.

'Adventurers help you think about being a Christian because they teach you things and help you think. When you are little you just do activities or hear stories. Adventurers start thinking about what it would be like being a real Christian. My next group, the Questers, will actually talk about what it is like to be a Christian.'

Youth Club

Table tennis at the URC Youth Club

Lots of children go to the Youth Club. More come each week and everyone is pleased to see them. There is no special ceremony when you join. You just go along. Ellie says, 'You don't have to belong to the Church to go to Youth Club. Sometimes my schoolfriend comes with me.' Lorna is also the leader of the Youth Club. She wants people to join. She writes to people saying, 'You're old enough now to come and join our club!'

Ellie says:

'Lorna is good at thinking of ideas. It's fun to have people like Lorna and it's nice to help them.'

Brownies

Joining Brownies means making a promise.

Emma is a new Brownie in Ellie's Six. Ellie led her through the ring of Brownies to the pool by the toadstool. The Brownie Guider told Emma she could choose whether to make the Brownie promise, but if she did, she would be expected to do her best to keep it always and everywhere.

Brownie promise badge

Emma said:

'I promise that I will do my best:
To love my God
To serve my Queen and Country and
To keep the Brownie Guide Law.'

The Guider pinned on Emma's new badge.

Ellie remembers her Brownie promise ceremony.

'I felt nervous because everyone was watching me and they were all saluting. I went a bit wrong and had to start again. The Brownie ceremony is like being baptized. You have to keep the promise. Perhaps I felt nervous when I was baptized. I was held by the minister and had a cross marked on my head. Mum says I cried my head off.'

What promise have you made?

What kind of occasion was it?

How hard have you tried to keep your promise?

11

Learning

I n each of the groups at the United Reformed Church, children learn, but what they learn is different.

Learning for Fun

At the Youth Club children learn skills for fun. They can try anything. Both the girls and the boys enjoy playing football and cooking.

Ellie's friends say they've tried lots of things, like jewellery-making, painting with food colouring and making fondant icing flowers.

Alastair enjoyed roller-booting the best. He's really expert.

Learning the Brownie Way

The Brownie Guider says:

'At Brownies we learn so we can gain badges. Sometimes Brownies work for interest badges on their own, sometimes together. At present we're all working on our Ramblers badge.'

Ellie's Six, the Gnomes, are trying hard to remember the Country Code.

Brownies carry out eight challenges to gain badges called 'Footpath,' 'Road' and 'Highway' badges. They call the work for these their 'learning and doing journeys'.

Learning about being Christian

The Adventurers group is different.

'You learn how to behave properly
and to understand more
grown up things. You learn
about God and to believe in God.
I think that's important.'

The children have been finding out about the **Communion** service. That is when Christians remember Jesus' last meal with his friends before he was crucified. Ellie's workbook says, 'Christians all over the world celebrate this special meal together.'

Communion

At the United Reformed Church the people pass the bread and wine from one to another as they sit in their seats. Everyone takes a cube of bread and a tiny glass of wine.

The church secretary brought the Communion silver into Junior Church for the children to look at.

Lorna says:

'It's important for the children to know what happens. They don't join in yet but perhaps one day they will.'

National Christian Education Council
BIBLE EXPLORATION 1994

A CHURCH LIKE OURS

Devised and illustrated
by Wendy Carolen

My name is _____

and my church is called _____

Communion
wine glasses
and bread

Which different people teach you things?

What will be the most useful do you think?

What is the most important for you to learn?

13

Believing and Worshipping

The inside of Ellie's church

| TEACHER'S RESOURCE BOOK | Photocopy sheets 5, 15, 16, 27 accompany this section |

Ellie and Nancy go to church most Sundays. Usually they sit with the other Junior Church members, but when the Brownies come to church for Church Parade, the girls join in with them.

Worship

The minister explains:

'**Worship** is when we set time apart to be with God. We don't do our normal thing. We come to a building to be quiet, to listen to God, to talk to God in **prayers** and to **praise** God.'

Christians usually want to tell God how wonderful they think He is.

Ellie believes that if you are a Christian:

'You should believe in God and Jesus, and believe that Jesus actually came from God.'

But she knows:

'Some people don't believe in God, like my friend at school. She doesn't believe in God and so she doesn't go to church.'

Nancy says:

'I come to church mainly for worship. God needs to know that I believe in Him and it's kind of friendly to worship Him.'

Nancy and her mum outside the church

Church Parade

Brownies carry the flag

When it's Church Parade the Brownies, Cubs, Scouts and Guides bring their flags to church. Children are chosen to carry them into the church. They hand them to the minister. The flags stay at the front till the end of the service. It's a way of showing that the children are keeping their promise to love God.

The Brownie Guider says:

'Parade is a good way for Brownies to learn about church life. Some of the children don't know what to expect. It's all a bit strange for them.'

The children are very welcome at church. As one of the adults says, 'I enjoy the service when it's Parade. When the minister talks to the children the adults can learn a lot too. It's nice to see them here.'

Everyone worships God together.

What do you think is worth believing in?

Is it God, or a person, or a really good idea?

How do you show you believe?

15

Prayer and Praise

One way Christians worship is to praise God. They tell Him the things they love about Him and thank Him for what He has done for them. It's a bit like when someone tells you that you have done well.

Singing Praises

At the United Reformed Church they sing praise to God in **hymns** or songs.

Each week the Junior Church and their leaders choose a hymn for the service.

Ellie explains:

'Before church we have a practice. One of our teachers, Gill, comes in with her guitar and we practise the songs to make sure we know them.'

During the service the children sing their hymn.

Gill says:

'We need to use all the things we do well to worship God and that includes music and song.'

BROWNIE BELLS

O Lord our God, Thy child-ren call,

Grant us Thy peace, And bless us all

A Brownie prayer

At the end of Brownie meetings, the girls sing Brownie Bells.

Brownie Bells isn't a hymn, it's a prayer that you sing. It sounds like bells ringing.

TEACHER'S RESOURCE BOOK Photocopy sheets 2, 17, 18, 28, 29, 31 accompany this section

Ellie's prayer

Each week one of the Brownies writes a prayer in the big prayer book. You can choose whether you want a turn or not.

Ellie's friend, Nancy, says:

'A prayer is a way of talking to God, telling him things and listening to him.'

Ellie wrote a prayer about homeless people.

'What started me thinking was a tape of a TV programme we saw at school. One of the children was talking about how we don't think about people who sleep in uncomfortable places. I had a think about what to write and then this is what I wrote.'

What else might Ellie write a prayer about?

Who do you ask to help you when you see a problem?

Dear Lord
When some people go home and get in bed they don't think about people who have no pillows or quilts to sleep on in cupboards under the stairs and in messy streets. Begers in the day beg for goods so please help these people find homes Lord,
Amen.
by Eleanor Hatcher.

Ellie's prayer

Ellie read her prayer in the Brownie meeting so everyone could join in.

The Bible

The Bible is a very important book for Christians. At the United Reformed Church an elder carries the Bible into the church at the beginning of the service. The congregation all stand up to show respect.

Reading the Bible

The elder places the Bible on a stand where it can be read. Each week a child is chosen to do one of the Bible readings. When Ellie is chosen, she practises at home with her mum.

When Nancy did a Bible reading she said:

'I was glad when the minister talked about my reading and explained it to everyone.'

TEACHER'S RESOURCE BOOK   Photocopy sheets 3, 4, 19, 20, 23 accompany this section

Learning about the Bible

In the Junior Church Adventurers group the children learn about the Bible. They like to find out what the Bible tells them about how to live.

'Our workbook asks us to read from the Bible. We're learning about the Corinthians and the letter **St Paul** wrote to them. Paul told the Corinthians what they were doing wrong and how to stop doing it.'

In the workbook it says, 'In his letter, Paul uses the idea of a human body to help the readers understand what he means. He said, "All the parts of a body are important. In the same way, every Christian is a necessary part of the church community." '

Everyone is different but useful to the church.

Is there a book you show respect to?

How?

Which book have you learnt most from?

In their group, the children drew round Matthew and painted his 'body'. Then they made speech bubbles to show what St Paul said.

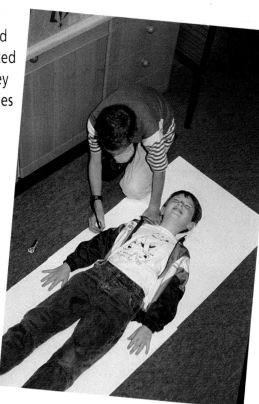

Elanie's bubble says, 'What do you think would happen if the different parts of the body decided not to work together?'

19

Living as a Christian

People who belong to religions think hard about how they should live. They may try to be kind or honest or hardworking, for instance. Christians get their ideas from the Bible.

The Bible says, 'Love your neighbour as yourself.' Christians try to do that by helping others. They try to be like Jesus.

A Christian Brownie

Some of the things Ellie does at Brownies are also just right for a Christian.

The Brownie motto is 'Lend a Hand' and the Brownie law says, 'A Brownie thinks of others before herself and does a good turn every day.'

LEND A HAND!

Ellie says:

'It means helping other people. I don't manage to do a good turn every day but I try.'

Some of the interest badges also teach Brownies how to help others.

Ellie says:

'I've got badges for accident prevention, crime prevention and safety in the home. For First Aid it's a red cross, like the cross in Christianity. I've been in a police car, an ambulance and a fire engine.'

TEACHER'S RESOURCE BOOK   Photocopy sheets 5, 8, 20, 21, 22, 31 accompany this section

Showing love

Another part of being a Christian is looking after the church. The Adventurers asked some of the adults what jobs they did in the church.

Mrs MacKay said:

'I shall be 81 in August and I still help with the cleaning and arranging flowers. I've always done what I could do to help.'

Then she explained why:

'I do it as a labour of love. I mean you're giving love by doing a job.'

Helping other people

The children say, 'At the United Reformed Church lots of appeals are put on to try to do work for God.'

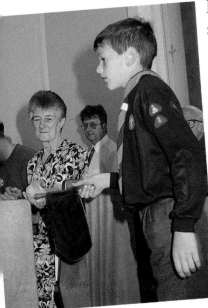

For example, there was a stall selling things to raise money for a home for elderly people.
   Another time, everyone collected food and useful things for a new hostel for homeless people. People also give money in the church services.

Ellie enjoys doing things to help other people:

'Doing something for someone else makes you feel happy – kind of satisfied.'

What kind of person do you want to be?

How do you work towards being that person?

Sharing

Town trail

A ll of the children's groups at the URC have fun together. When you have fun together you get to know each other really well. Then you can help each other when things go wrong.

Doing things together

Brownies play games and go outdoors to enjoy themselves. Once they went out on a town trail to hunt for different buildings.

Another time the Junior Church went for a picnic in a park with a river. There were fairground rides and rowing boats.

Youth Club activities are always fun. One evening they had a sports skills competition. They tried lots of different activities and kept score to see who would be the champion. Alastair won! They finished off with a barbecue, cooking hot dogs and squishy marshmallows.

Cooking hot dogs on the barbecue

TEACHER'S RESOURCE BOOK

Photocopy sheets 13, 23, 24, 32 accompany this section

Sharing means caring

Sharing isn't only having fun. The children heard about a child who was in another country in prison, just because he was a Christian. They all sent Christmas cards to show they cared about him.

Brownie Thinking Day

Once a year Brownies have **Thinking Day** to think about the World Guide Family. Often there are services at church and special Thinking Day meetings.

Brownies pray for their sisters around the world.

'We give money to help through the Thinking Day Fund.'

World badge

Sharing a special meal

The Communion Service is a way of sharing a special meal with Christians everywhere.

The Adventurers' workbook says, 'Not all the churches use bread and wine at communion. Churches in some countries use coconut milk, grape juice, rice or chapattis. People can receive communion in their homes, in hospital – even on the battle-field or in prison.'

Communion is a time when all Christians feel especially close to God and to each other. Sometimes the adults hold the children's hands. It helps them all feel strong and ready to live in the Christian way.

What do you do with your friends?

How does it join you together?

Do you have any 'friends' that you haven't ever seen?

23

Dean's Groups

Dean spends a lot of time with the church groups he belongs to. He and his friends have good fun and they learn about being a Christian as well.

Belonging to the Salvation Army

Dean and his friends wear a uniform to show they belong to the Salvation Army.

'We wear blue trousers, a white shirt, tie and badge. Everyone can see who we are and what we do. If I didn't wear a uniform I couldn't belong to the Singing Company or the Young People's Band.'

The uniform stands for war against wrong-doing and is a sign to show that the person wearing it is a member of the Salvation Army and a Christian.

Sometimes Dean joins the adults when they march through the streets singing and playing.

Being a Junior Soldier

When Dean was 7 he chose to become a Junior Soldier. On Sunday mornings he goes to church and Sunday School. In the afternoon he goes to another Sunday School meeting before joining the adults again at church.

Dean says:

'You have to decide you want to be a Junior Soldier. I go to church every Sunday unless I'm ill or on holiday. I never just miss it for the sake of it.'

TEACHER'S RESOURCE BOOK Photocopy sheets 6, 11, 15, 25, 26 accompany this section

The Choir

Dean also belongs to The Young People's Singing Company. They show how much they love Jesus through song. Singing is a way of praising God.

The choir leader, Beverley, says:

'The children are excited and stimulated by the Singing Company. They often find it very hard work, but it is rewarding.'

Choir practice

The Youth Club

Dean belongs to the Youth Club. No-one wears uniform here. Sometimes they play snooker. They can buy sweets and drinks. Dean likes to play with the computer best of all.

Junior Soldiers sometimes bring friends from school to join in the fun.

Dean's Youth Club members

What is so important you wouldn't miss it?

When did you stand up for something you believe important?

How do people know what you belong to?

Celebrating

Sunday is a special time for Dean and his friends. It is an important time for Christians everywhere to get together to worship and celebrate God.

Dean in church

'We sing and my mum and dad do sermons. They talk about God. The stories at church are quite good. When my mum and dad do sermons they think about them and they say things about them.'

Everyone is happy and friendly. They enjoy praising God by singing. Dean is learning to play the tenor horn. He will play it in the People's Band when he is good enough. The Singing Company sings at every Sunday meeting for the adults.

The church is quite full and most people are in uniform.

The Bible rests on a table at the front of the hall. This shows that it is a very important book for Christians. When someone reads a passage they use a small copy.

TEACHER'S RESOURCE BOOK Photocopy sheets 7, 18, 20, 27, 28 accompany this section

The Young People's anniversary

Tonight has been very special. Dean and the other Junior Soldiers put on a show for the adults.

One of the officers, Glenys, explains:

'We're very keen on putting children on show in the Army. They have two special weekends of their own when they perform. They do drama and they're in the choir or the band. They play their musical instruments. They might recite or something like that.'

The performance

Everyone was rather nervous. Dean played a tune on his tenor horn. He need not have worried because he played well. The audience gave him a good clap.

Then Dean acted as a newspaper reporter in a little play. The play was to help people think about being well prepared.

Alison, a Junior Soldier, has written the words and composed the music for a song. She taught her song to the Singing Company and they all sang it.

The audience enjoyed the show very much.

What do you think is worth praising?

When were you part of a celebration?

What did you do?

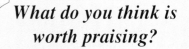

ALISON'S SONG

'Rejoice, rejoice and be glad.
No need to be sad
'cause God is there,
you're in His care.
Rejoice, rejoice and be glad.'

Learning in Different Ways

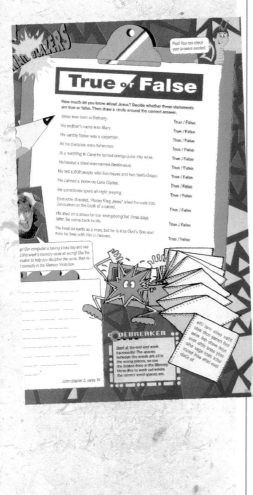

After the Sunday meeting with the adults Dean goes to Sunday School with other young people who are Junior Soldiers.

Glenys is in charge. She is called the Young People's Sergeant Major.

Glenys says:

'Our kids are really wonderful and we have a good time together. The aim is to help people to understand about God's love and about the importance of having Jesus in their lives.'

Learning is fun

The young people pray, play games and sing songs. The Young People's Band plays for them.

Glenys, or one of the children, reads a passage from the Bible and then they talk about it.

Later they split up into smaller groups. Dean is in Claire's group. They have fun doing quizzes and playing games. Everyone learns about the Bible.

TEACHER'S RESOURCE BOOK	Photocopy sheets 23, 29, 30 accompany this section

Afternoon Sunday School

Dean goes to Sunday School meeting on Sunday afternoon. This is the time when the Junior Soldiers learn a lot about being a member of the Salvation Army, and about being a follower of Jesus.

Dean is working hard for his Silver Award. He has passed his Bronze Award. It took nearly two years to do all the projects and activities. He had to do things like lead prayer at a Sunday meeting, and invite someone new to the meeting.

Junior Soldiers'
AWARD

This award was presented to

Dean Heeley

Corps Coventry City   Date 21.3.95

Divisional Youth Secretary

Commanding Officer

'When I got my Bronze Award I felt good because I passed my first award. I was given a letter and a wreath to put on my badge.'

The Lord's Prayer

The children have been learning about the Lord's Prayer. Dean and his friends fill in a worksheet to show that they know the prayer; then they look at a bit of it and put the right words in the spaces. They work together to answer the questions.

GIVE US THIS DAY OUR DAILY BREAD

In this space draw some food you **like** to eat, and some food which makes you healthy. When we pray 'Give us this day our daily bread,' we are asking for the food we _____

Before we can get the food we need, both God and man must do his part.

The wheat for bread will only grow in the right _____
There must be the right kind of _____ LOSI
The soil must be ploughed and harrowed by a _____ ETAMICL
The seed needs _____ RNAI and _____ SNU to grow.
When the seed is _____ TSNCEIITS tell the farmer the best kinds of seed
When the seed is harvested the _____ LLMIER turns it to
flour and the _____ KEARB makes it into bread.

Put a circle around every word you have written which tells God's part.
Put a line under every word you have written which tells man's part.

What do you learn in the groups that you belong to?

Are you working towards any goal?

What is it?

Caring for others

J unior Soldiers learn to care for people. Dean had to learn to greet people when they arrived at the Sunday Meetings as part of his Bronze Award.

Another time he made a card and sent it to someone who was sick.

Choir practice

Making people happy

When the Singing Company choir rehearses, Beverley, the leader, always tells them a story. One evening she told them how she went to an Army corps in another town and a Junior Soldier talked to her and made her feel very welcome. This made her happy because she didn't know anyone. She said she hoped everyone would do the same for visitors who came to their corps.

Dean often goes with the choir to sing at an Old People's Home. Many of the old people aren't well enough to go out. They really enjoy listening to the children and they join in with the singing.

Ways of caring

Junior Soldiers learn to care for people in different ways.

Every week Dean brings some of his pocket money he has saved to Junior Soldiers.

Dean says:

*'This is called a "**cartridge**". It helps to pay for things like books.'*

Every year there is an Appeal when the adults go from door to door to collect money. Junior Soldiers bring money they have saved by giving up a treat. This money helps to care for people in this country and abroad.

THE SALVATION ARMY
WILLIAM BOOTH Founder

Young People's Register and Cartridge Record

Year 1995

Corps

Homeless people

Dean has also been out with his parents some nights to give homeless people hot soup.

William Booth, the Salvation Army founder, said that there was no point in talking to people about God if they were starving. For over a hundred years the Salvation Army has provided hostels for homeless people and has looked after the poor all over the world.

What thoughtful thing have you done for someone else?

Who else might Dean want to help?

Glossary

baptized Being welcomed into the Church

Bible The Christian holy book

Brownies An organization for girls founded by Lord and Lady Baden-Powell

cartridge A weekly amount of money given to the church

Christian Someone who follows the teachings of Jesus of Nazareth

church All the Christians who have ever lived; the building where Christians worship; a group of Christian people who worship God together

citadel A place of worship in the Salvation Army

Communion A service when Christians share special food and feel close to God and to each other

corps A local group of the Salvation Army

elder A chosen leader in the United Reformed Church

hymn A song sung to God

Jesus The founder of Christianity, worshipped by Christians

Major A commanding officer in the Salvation Army

minister A person who has studied Christianity and is chosen by the church as a leader

officers Trained leaders in the Salvation Army

praise Speaking and singing to tell God how wonderful He is or telling God how glad you are about Him

prayer Talking to God and listening to Him

service A meeting for worship

soldiers Full members of the Salvation Army

St Paul An early Christian who explained about Jesus and how to be a good Christian in his letters

Thinking Day A day when Brownies think about the World Guide family

worship Setting time aside for God

Index